BEGINNING PIANO SOLO

SONGS OF THE BEATLES

ISBN 978-1-4234-9468-7

HAL•LEONARD®
CORPORATION
7777 W. BLUEMOUND RD. P.O. BOX 13819 MILWAUKEE, WI 53213

Visit Hal Leonard Online at
www.halleonard.com

AND I LOVE HER

Words and Music by JOHN LENNON
and PAUL McCARTNEY

Moderately

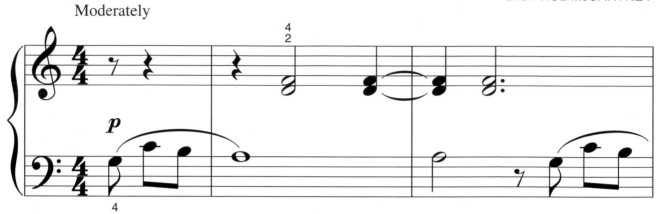

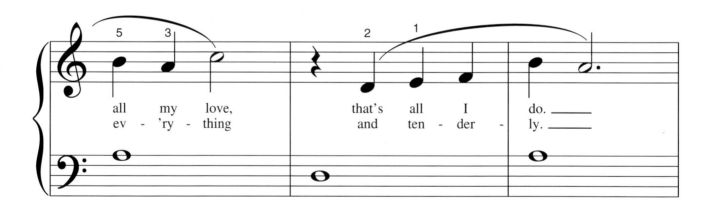

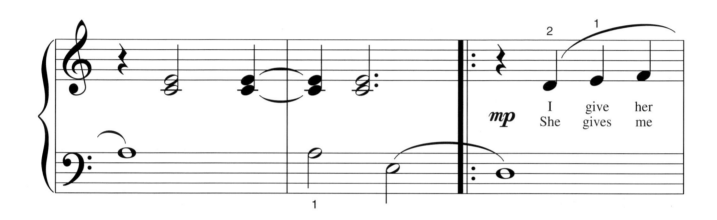

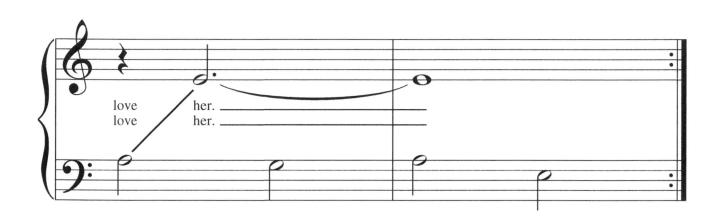

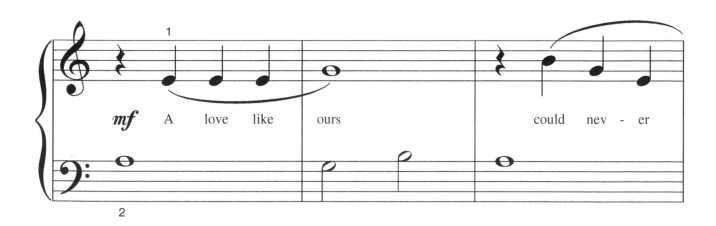

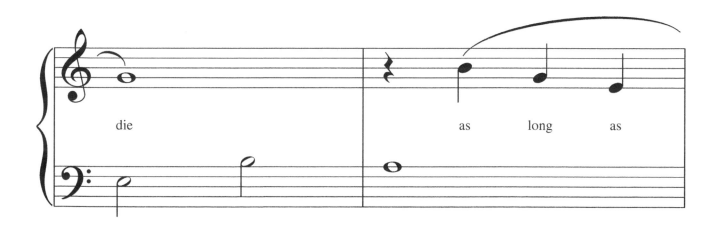

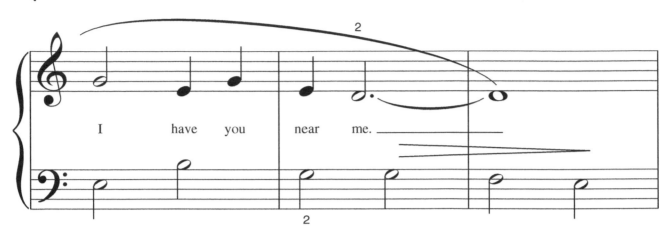

I have you near me.

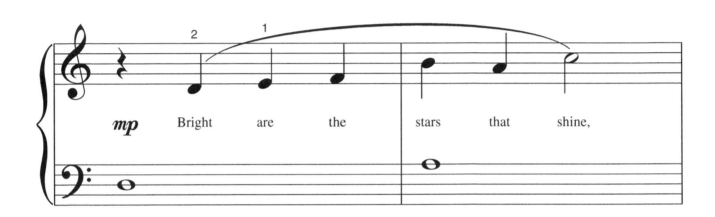

mp Bright are the stars that shine,

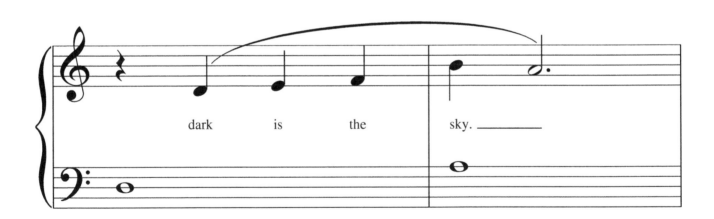

dark is the sky.

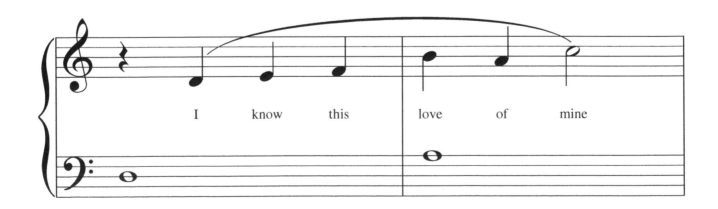

I know this love of mine

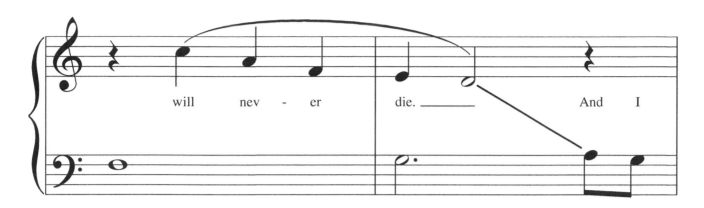

will nev - er die. _____ And I

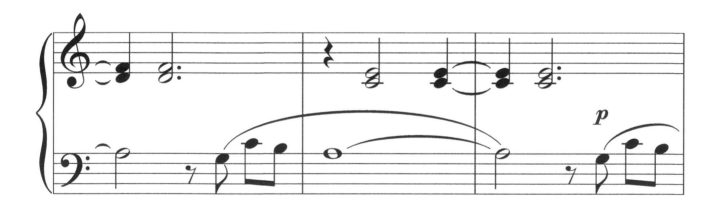

love her. _____

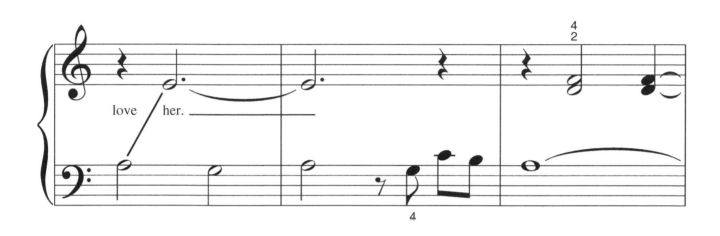

BLACKBIRD

Words and Music by JOHN LENNON
and PAUL McCARTNEY

Slowly

1., 3. Black - bird sing - ing in the dead of night,
2. Black - bird sing - ing in the dead of night,

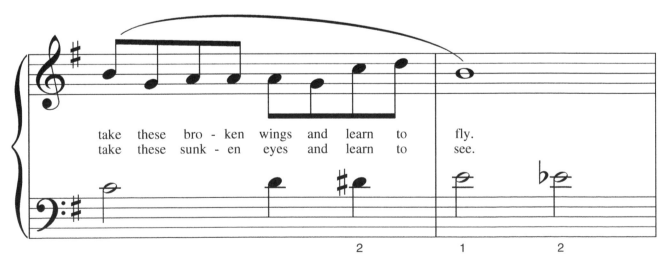

take these bro - ken wings and learn to fly.
take these sunk - en eyes and learn to see.

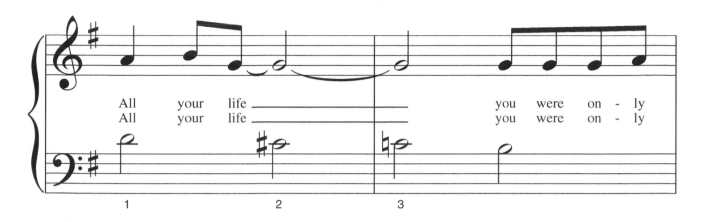

All   your   life _____   you   were   on - ly
All   your   life _____   you   were   on - ly

1   2   3

To Coda ⊕ | 1.

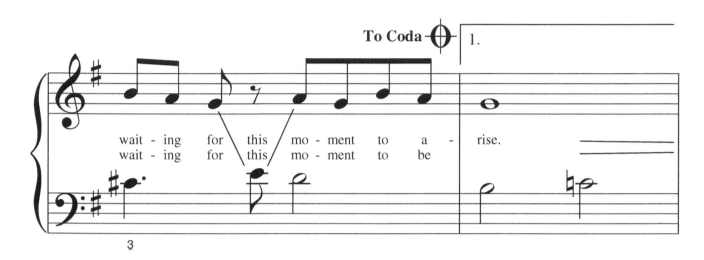

wait - ing   for   this   mo - ment   to   a -   rise.
wait - ing   for   this   mo - ment   to   be

3

2.

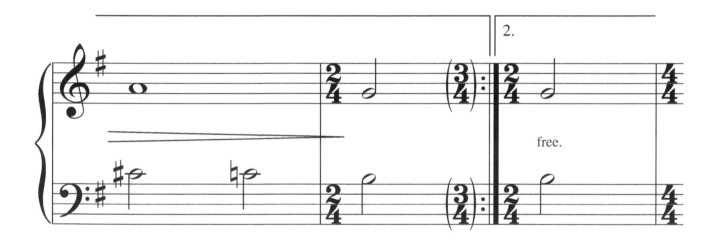

free.

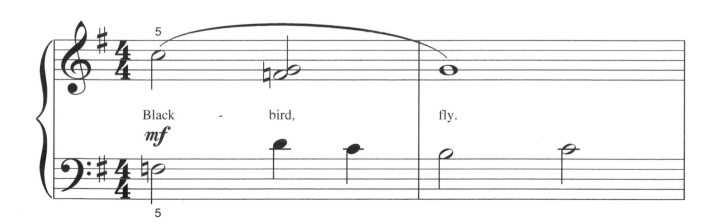

Black -   bird,   fly.

mf

5

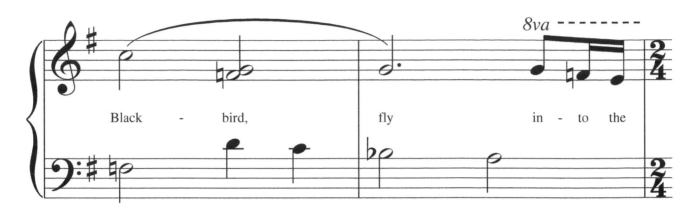

Black - bird, fly in - to the

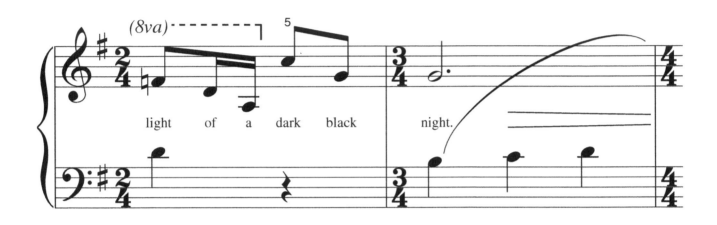

light of a dark black night.

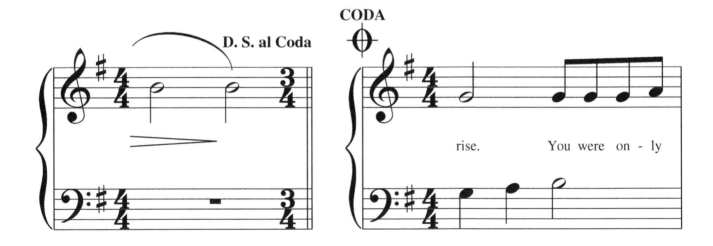

D. S. al Coda

CODA

rise. You were on - ly

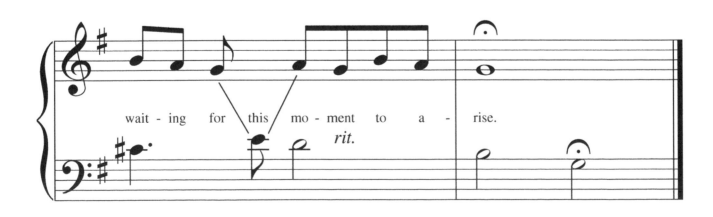

wait - ing for this mo - ment to a - rise.

rit.

GOOD DAY SUNSHINE

Words and Music by JOHN LENNON
and PAUL McCARTNEY

10

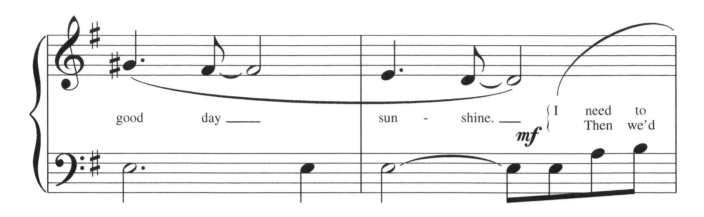

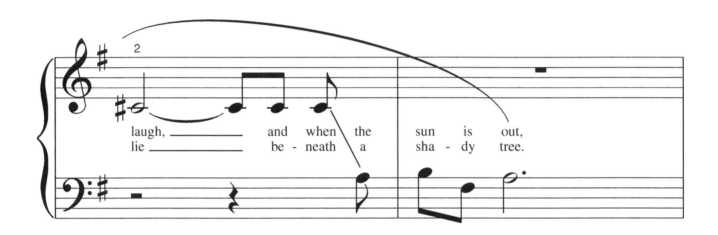

I'm in love, and it's a sun - ny day. ___
I'm so proud to know that she is mine. ___

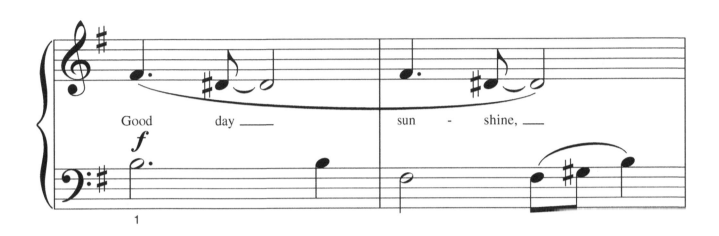

Good day ___ sun - shine, ___

To Coda

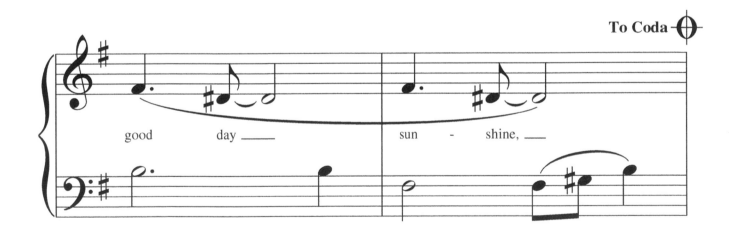

good day ___ sun - shine, ___

good day ___ sun - shine. ___ We take a

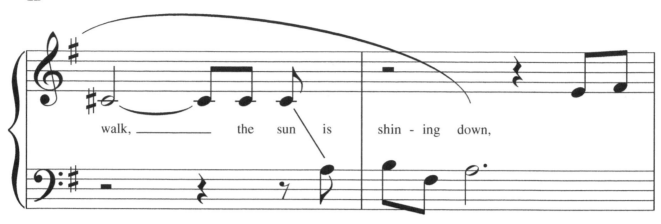

walk, _____ the sun is shin - ing down,

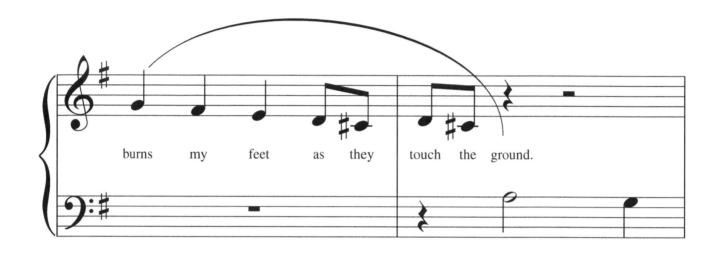

burns my feet as they touch the ground.

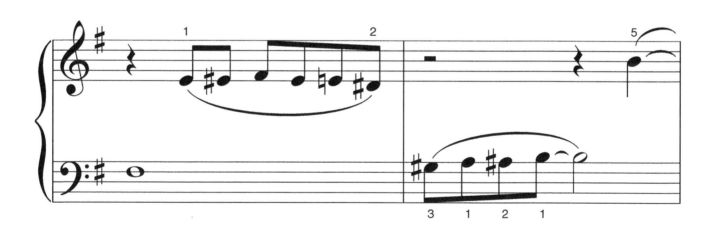

D.S. al Coda

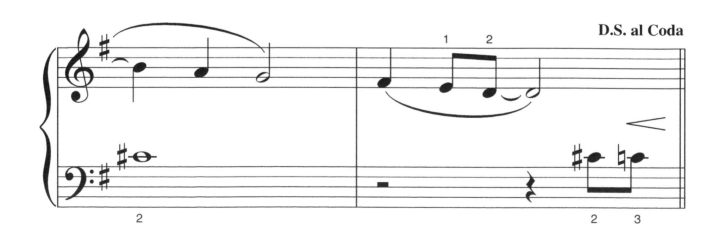

CODA

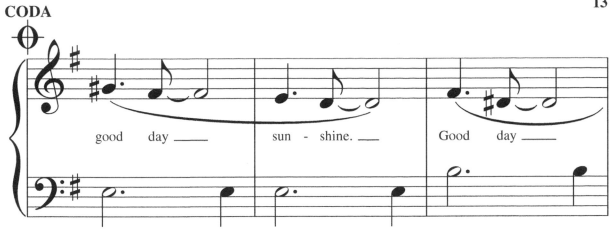

good day _____ sun - shine. _____ Good day _____

sun - shine, _____ good day _____ sun - shine, _____

good day _____ sun - shine. _____ Good day _____

mf

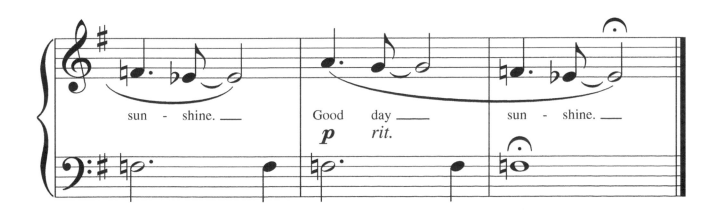

sun - shine. _____ Good day _____ sun - shine. _____

p *rit.*

GOOD NIGHT

Words and Music by JOHN LENNON
and PAUL McCARTNEY

Slowly and dreamily

Now it's time to say good night. Good night,

sleep tight. Now the sun turns out his light.

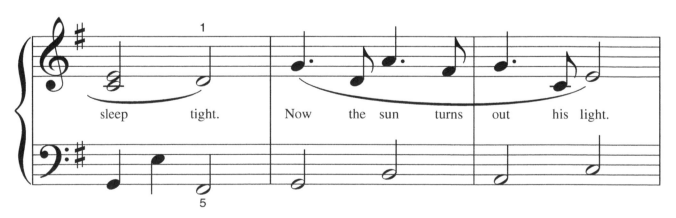

15

Good night, sleep tight.

Dream sweet dreams for me.

Dreams sweet dreams for you.

Close your eyes and I'll close mine.

16

Good night, sleep tight.

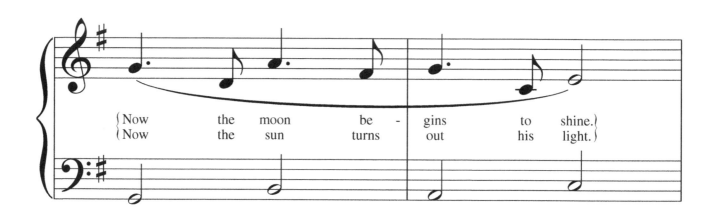

{Now the moon be - gins to shine.}
{Now the sun turns out his light.}

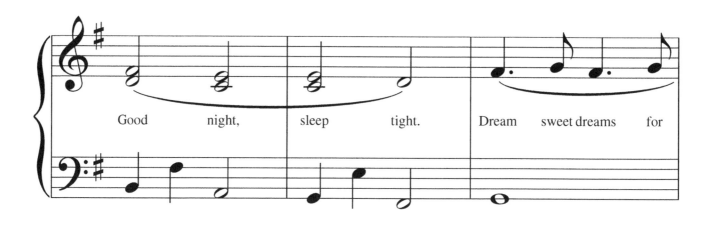

Good night, sleep tight. Dream sweet dreams for

me, dream sweet dreams for

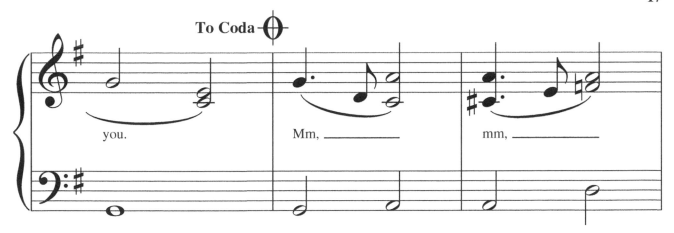

MICHELLE

Words and Music by JOHN LENNON
and PAUL McCARTNEY

Gentle Ballad

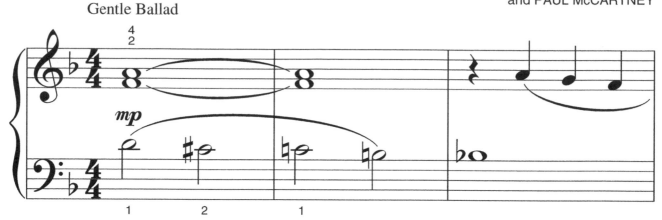

Mi - chelle, ma belle,

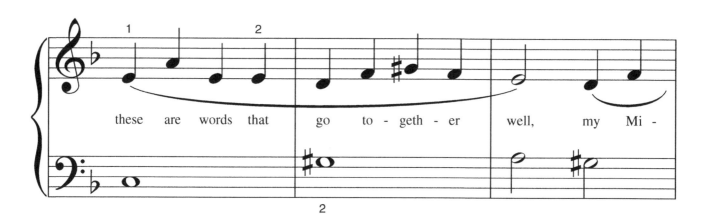

these are words that go to-geth-er well, my Mi-

chelle. Mi - chelle, ma belle,
Mi - chelle, ma belle,
I love you, *Instrumental*

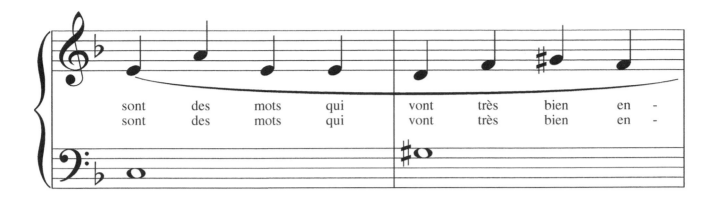

sont   des   mots   qui   vont   très   bien   en -
sont   des   mots   qui   vont   très   bien   en -

semble,   très   bien   en -   semble.
semble,   très   bien   en -   semble.

mf
End Instrumental

1
I
I
I

love   you,   I   love   you,   I   love   you,
need   to,   I   need   to,   I   need   to,
want you,   I   want   you, I   want   you,

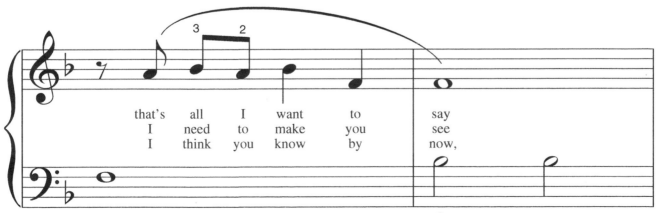

3   2

that's   all   I   want   to   say
I   need   to   make   you   see
I   think you   know   by   now,

un - til   I   find   a   way _____   I   will
oh,   what   you   mean   to   me. _____   Un -
I'll   get   to   you   some - how. _____   Un -

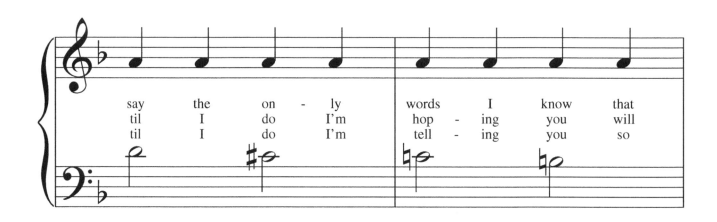

say   the   on - ly   words   I   know   that
til   I   do   I'm   hop - ing   you   will
til   I   do   I'm   tell - ing   you   so

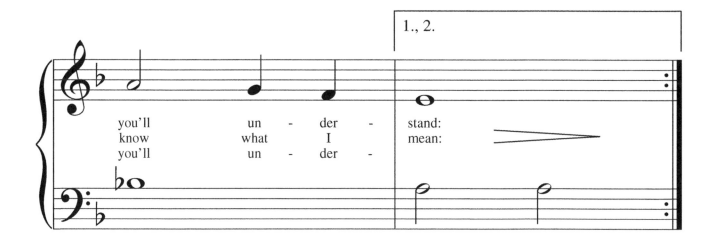

1., 2.

you'll   un - der - stand:
know   what   I   mean:
you'll   un - der -

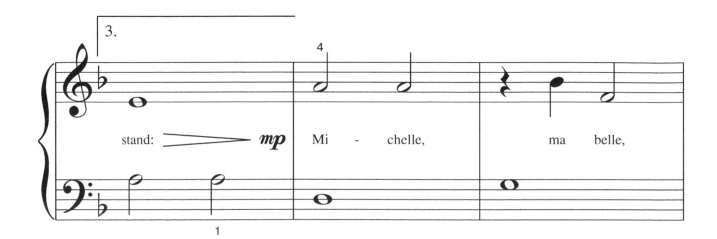

3.

stand: _____ *mp*   Mi - chelle,   ma   belle,

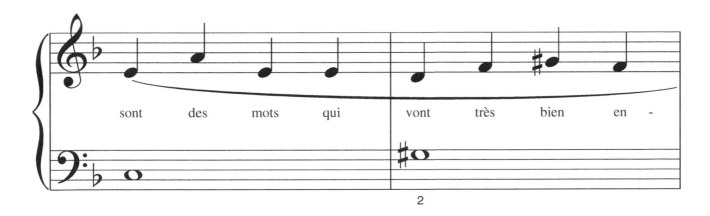

sont des mots qui vont très bien en -

semble, très bien en - semble. And I will

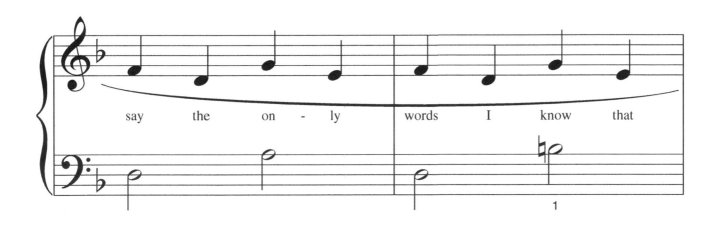

say the on - ly words I know that

you'll un - der - stand, my Mi - chelle.

rit.

WHEN I'M SIXTY-FOUR

Words and Music by JOHN LENNON
and PAUL McCARTNEY

Moderately

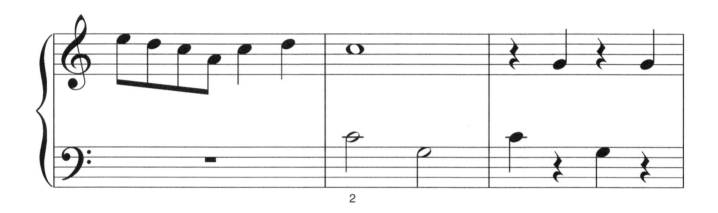

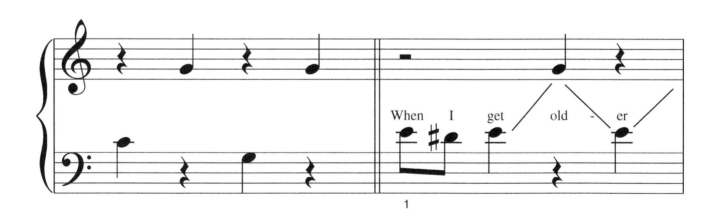

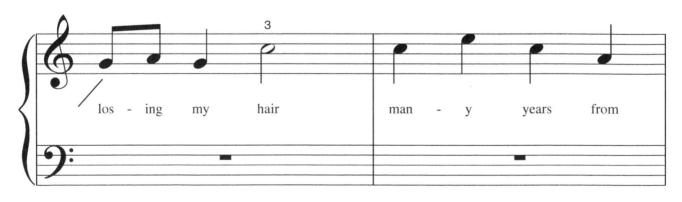

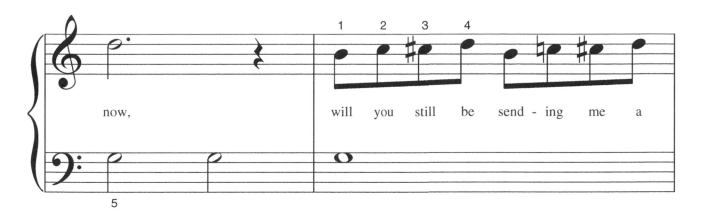

now,   will you still be send - ing me a

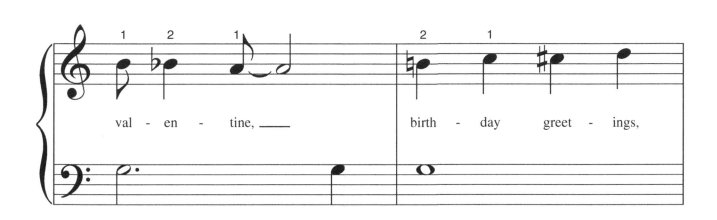

val - en - tine, ___   birth - day greet - ings,

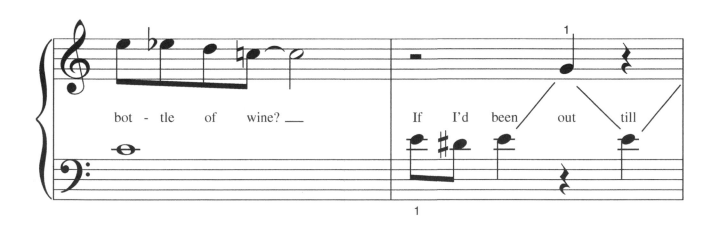

bot - tle of wine? ___   If I'd been out till

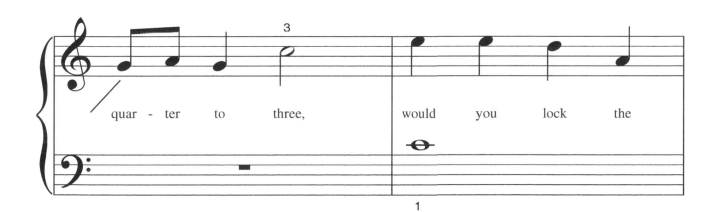

quar - ter to three,   would you lock the

24

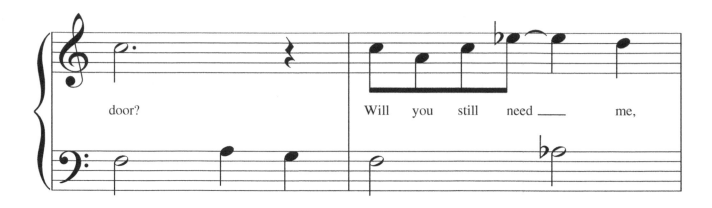

door?   Will   you   still   need ____   me,

will   you   still   feed ____   me,   when   I'm   six - ty -

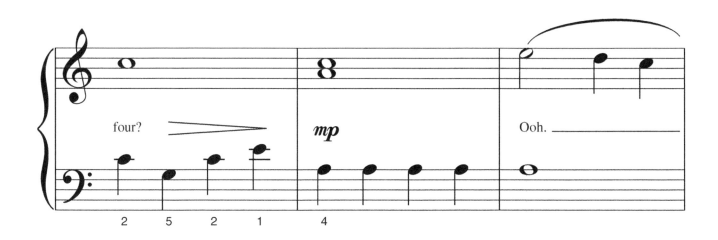

four?   *mp*   Ooh. _____

2   5   2   1   4

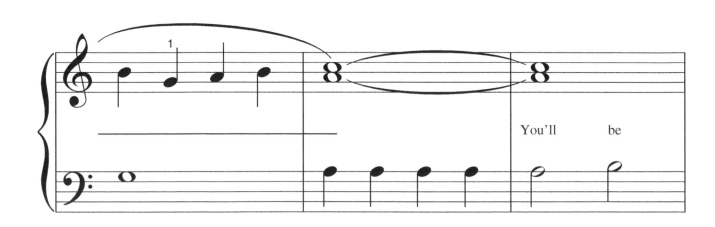

1   You'll   be

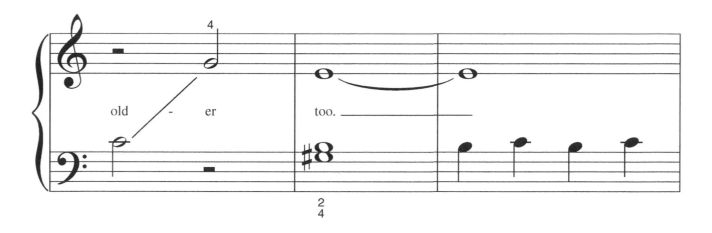

old - er too.

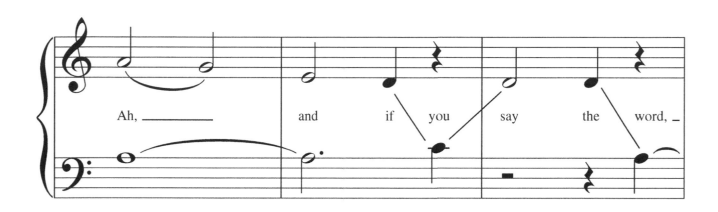

Ah, _____ and if you say the word, _

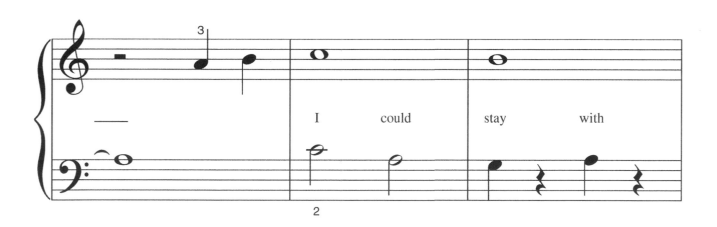

_____ I could stay with

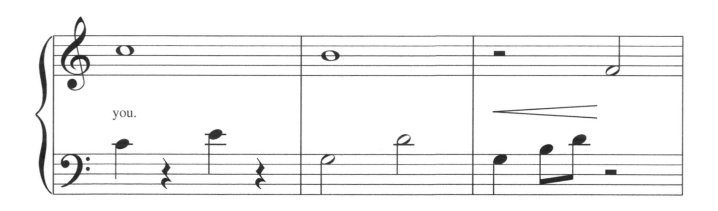

you.

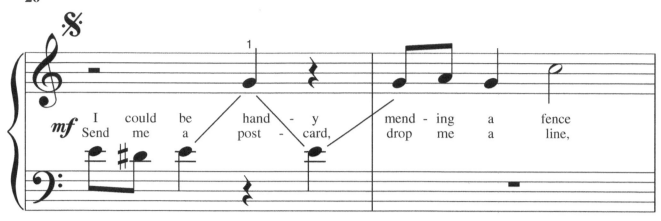

I could be hand - y mend - ing a fence
Send me a post - card, drop me a line,

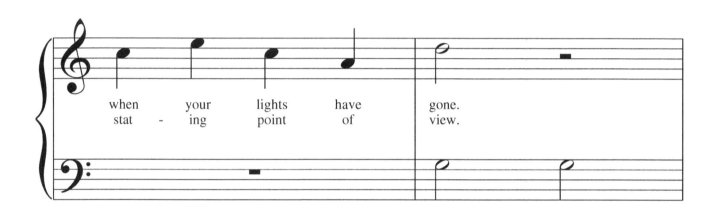

when your lights have gone.
stat - ing point of view.

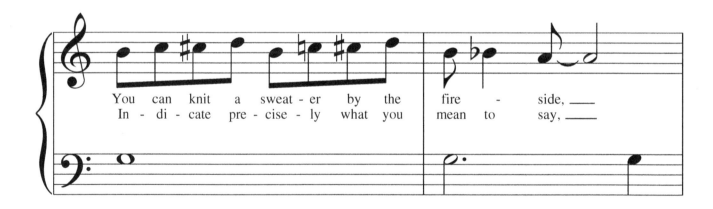

You can knit a sweat - er by the fire - side, ____
In - di - cate pre - cise - ly what you mean to say, ____

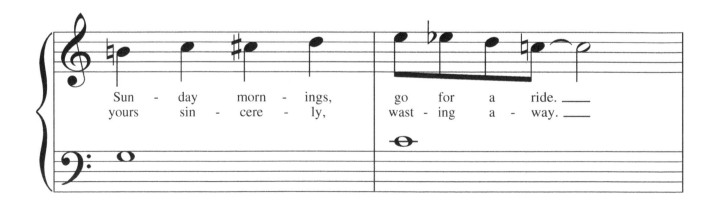

Sun - day morn - ings, go for a ride. ____
yours sin - cere - ly, wast - ing a - way. ____

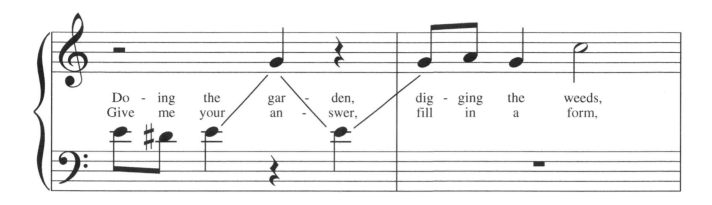

Do - ing the gar - den, dig - ging the weeds,
Give me your an - swer, fill in a form,

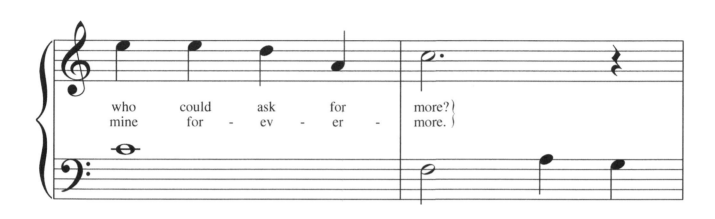

who could ask for more?
mine for - ev - er - more.

Will you still need ___ me, will you still feed ___ me,

To Coda ⊕

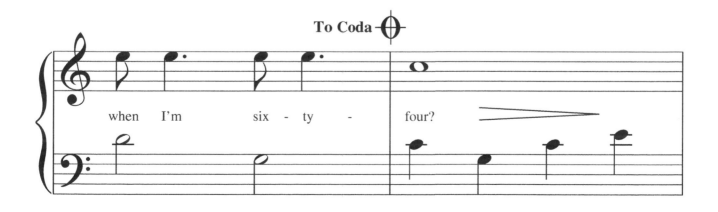

when I'm six - ty - four?

28

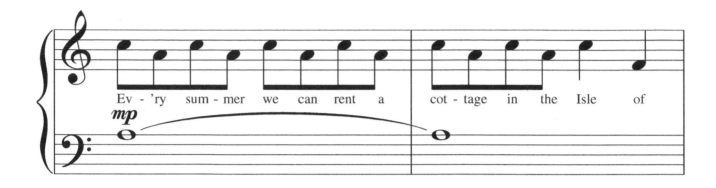

Ev - 'ry sum - mer we can rent a cot - tage in the Isle of
mp

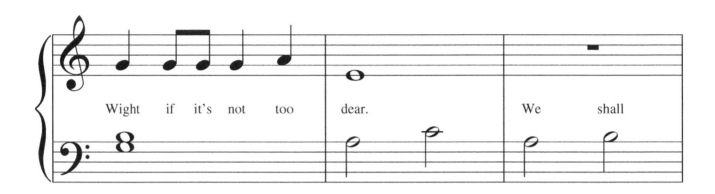

Wight if it's not too dear. We shall

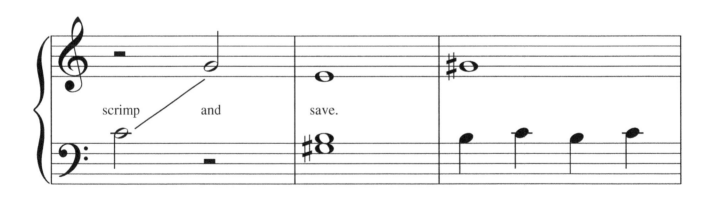

scrimp   and   save.

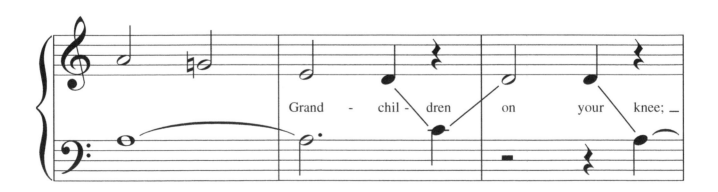

Grand - chil - dren   on   your   knee; __

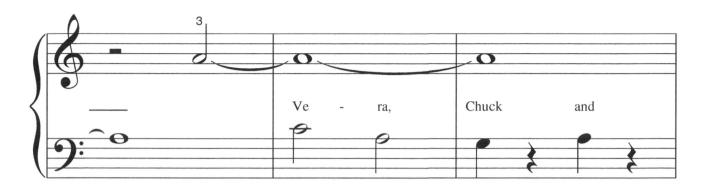

D.S. al Coda

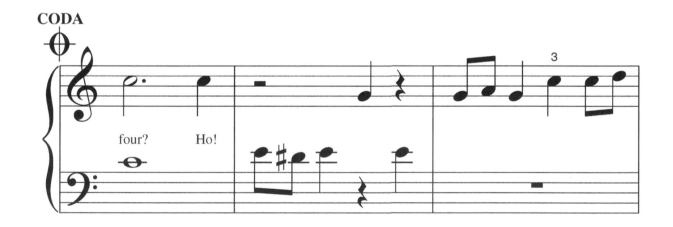

CODA

I WANT TO HOLD YOUR HAND

Words and Music by JOHN LENNON
and PAUL McCARTNEY

Moderate Rock

Oh, yeah,

I'll _____ tell you some - thing
please _____ say to me _____

I think you'll un - der - stand. When
you'll let me be your man. And

I _____ say that some - thing
please _____ say to me _____

I want to hold your hand,
you'll let me hold your hand.

I want to hold your hand, _____
Now let me hold your hand, _____

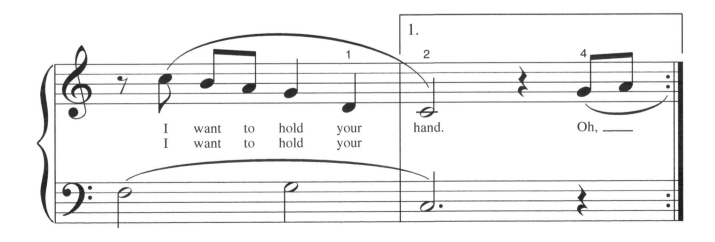

I want to hold your hand.
I want to hold your

Oh, _____

32

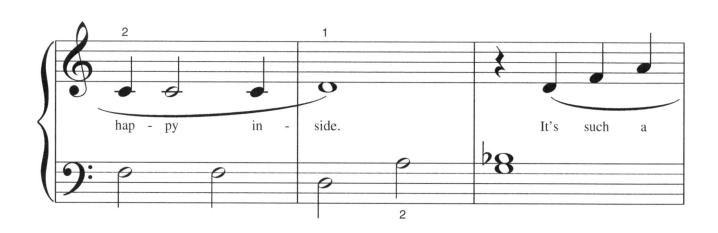

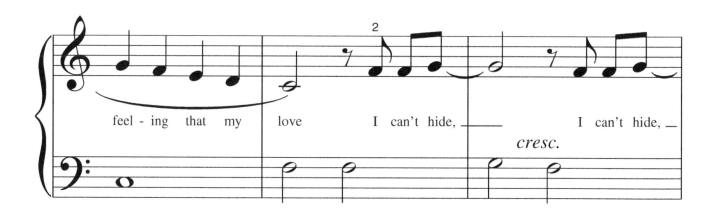

you _____ got that some - thing

3
I think you'll un - der - stand. When

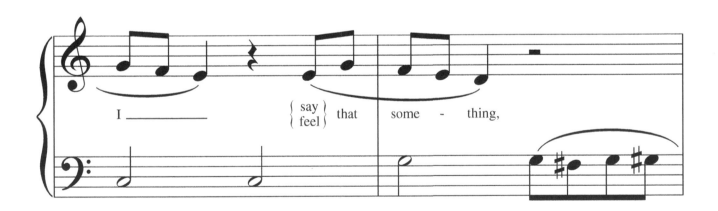

I _____ { say / feel } that some - thing,

I want to hold your hand,

I want to hold your hand, _____

1.

I want to hold your hand.

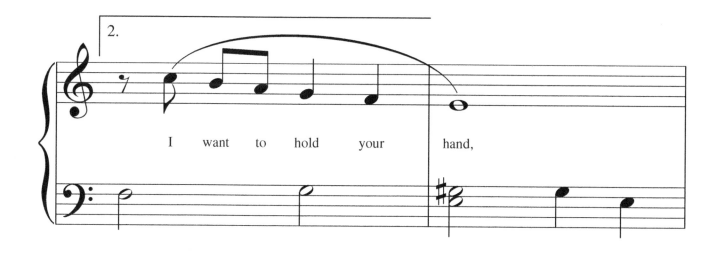

2.

I want to hold your hand,

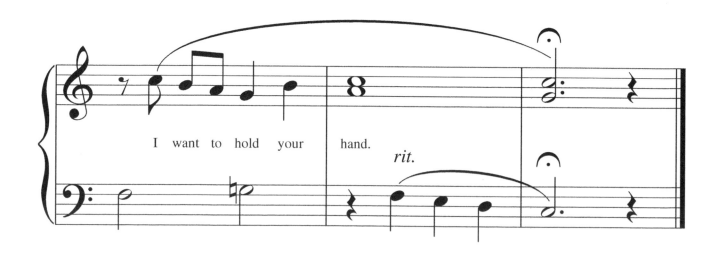

I want to hold your hand.

rit.

YELLOW SUBMARINE

Words and Music by JOHN LENNON
and PAUL McCARTNEY

36

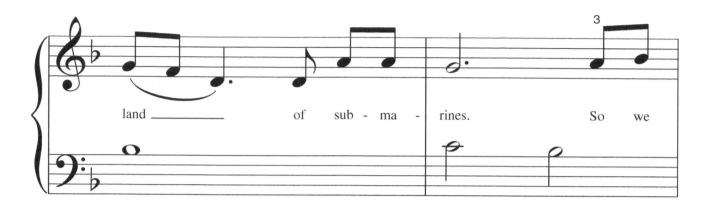

land _____ of sub - ma - rines. So we

sailed _____ up to the sun till we

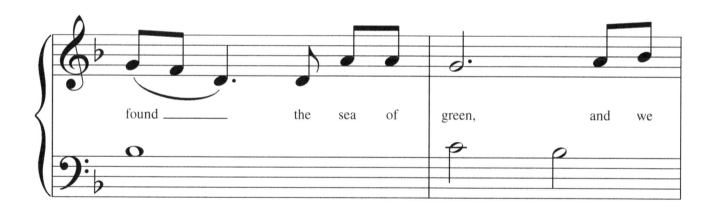

found _____ the sea of green, and we

lived _____ be - neath the waves in our

yel - low sub - ma - rine.

We all live in a yel - low sub - ma - rine,

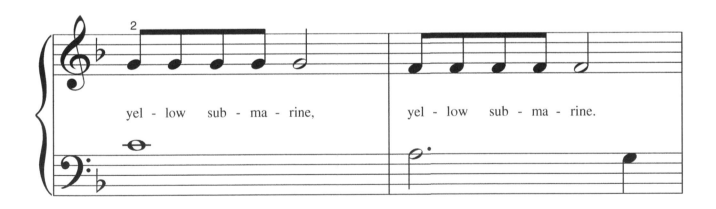

yel - low sub - ma - rine, yel - low sub - ma - rine.

We all live in a yel - low sub - ma - rine,

38

yel - low sub - ma - rine,   yel - low sub - ma - rine. { And our
                                                          { As we

mf

friends _____ are all on board   man - y
live _____ a life of ease   ev - 'ry

more of them   live next door.   And the
one of us has   all we need.   Sky of

1.

band _____ be - gins to play:
blue _____ and sea of

f

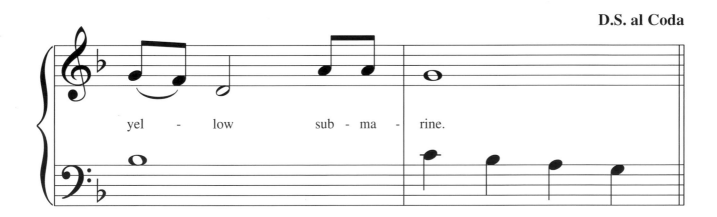

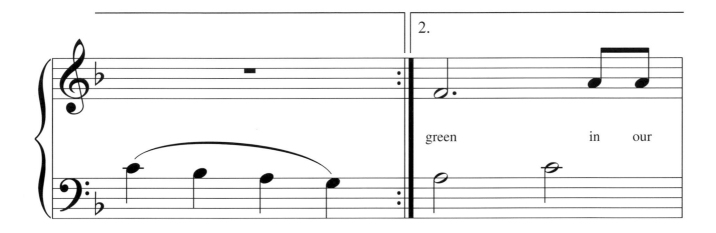

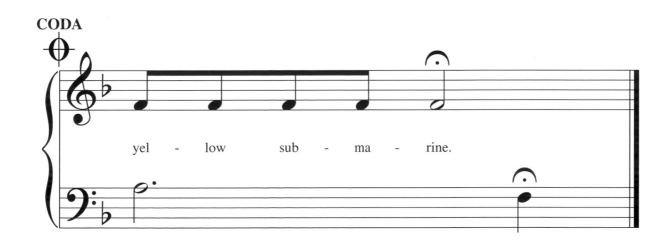